decorating
cookies

decorating cookies

Annie Rigg with photography by Kate Whitaker

RYLAND
PETERS
& SMALL

LONDON NEW YORK

Design and photographic art direction Steve Painter
Senior editor Céline Hughes
Head of production Patricia Harrington
Art director Leslie Harrington
Publishing director Alison Starling

First published in 2010 by
Ryland Peters & Small
20–21 Jockey's Fields
London WC1R 4BW

519 Broadway, 5th Floor
New York, NY 10012

www.rylandpeters.com

The recipes in this book have been published previously by Ryland Peters & Small in *Decorating Cakes & Cookies* and *Easy Cookies*

10 9 8 7 6 5 4 3 2 1

All recipes by Annie Rigg except Classic Oat Cookies, Extra-crunchy Peanut Butter Cookies, Classic Chocolate Chip Cookies, Double Chocolate and Pecan Cookies, and Mocha Kisses, all by Linda Collister.

All photographs by Kate Whitaker except pages 53, 54, 56, 57, 59, 60, 62: Diana Miller; and pages 8, 9: Peter Cassidy

ISBN for kit: 978-1-84975-057-8

Printed and bound in China

• All spoon measurements are level, unless otherwise specified.

• Ovens should be preheated to the specified temperature. Recipes in this book were tested using a regular oven. If using a fan-assisted oven, follow the manufacturer's instructions for adjusting temperatures.

• All eggs are large, unless otherwise specified. Recipes containing raw or partially cooked egg should not be served to the very young, very old, anyone with a compromised immune system or pregnant women.

contents

creative cookies

Baking a batch of cookies is the best antidote to a rainy day. In fact, pulling a tray of just-baked chocolate chip cookies from the oven is akin to a warm hug, a glass of wine or a hot bath for its therapeutic effects. But the best thing about cookies is that there's so much you can do with them.

With just a handful of ingredients, you've got the potential to make little morsels of oaty, chocolatey or nutty biscuits, perfect with that morning cup of coffee, an after-lunch sweet treat, or an afternoon snack attack.

Sometimes the urge strikes to do something creative – perhaps for a friend's birthday present, or because you have an afternoon to fritter away. That's when cookies come into their own because you can use them as a blank canvas on which to create something pretty, fun or stunning – and then eat it too! There is so much you can do with a simple cookie base that you can spend hours discovering the joys of piping bags, icing, food colouring and sugar paste. Whether you need a quick decorating idea (like the 'stained glass' cookies opposite) or a dazzling design with a special theme, the possibilities are endless.

You don't need any great skill or even to possess a huge array of fancy kitchen equipment to make something unique. Most of the recipes in this book use standard equipment. All you need is a couple of piping bags, a selection of nozzles, a few assorted cookie cutters and a rainbow of food colouring pastes. All of these are now widely available in most cookshops or from online suppliers (see page 63). And there are so many beautiful sprinkles and sparkles for the home baker to use that it seems crazy not to make the most of them.

Most of the recipes in this book use one of two simple cookie doughs as their base so once you've mastered those, you can concentrate on honing your decorating skills. There are also some easy-to-follow steps to guide you through the decorating techniques. There's a recipe for you however wobbly your baking skills might be, starting with simple gingerbread men (and women) right up to the fabulously decorated shoes on pages 34–35.

These cookies are perfect as gifts, for that special party or just to cheer up a friend. How fabulous would it be to give your loved one a batch of Mint Chocolate Kisses instead of an unimaginative bunch of roses or box of chocolates? Go on, get out those sprinkles and make someone smile.

basics

You will need to chill this cookie dough for a good couple of hours before rolling out and shaping into cookies. The cookies will keep, unfrosted, for 3 days in an airtight box. If frosted, they should be eaten within 24 hours.

basic vanilla cookies

225 g/15 tablespoons unsalted butter, softened

225 g/1 generous cup caster sugar

1 egg, beaten

½ teaspoon vanilla extract

a pinch of salt

450 g/3½ cups plain/all-purpose flour, sifted, plus extra for dusting

Cream together the butter and sugar until light and creamy. Add the beaten egg, vanilla and salt and mix well.

Gradually add the flour and mix until incorporated. Bring together into a dough, then flatten into a disc. Wrap in clingfilm/plastic wrap and refrigerate for 2 hours.

Roll the dough out on a lightly floured work surface to a thickness of 4 mm/⅛ inch, then turn to the relevant recipe.

Remember that once you have stamped out the shapes required in the individual recipes, you can gather the remaining dough together into a ball and re-roll to make more shapes. The shapes will then need to be refrigerated for a further 15 minutes before baking.

gingerbread cookies

Like the Basic Vanilla Cookies, these will keep unfrosted for 3 days in an airtight box. If frosted, they should be eaten within 24 hours.

375 g/a scant 3 cups plain/all-purpose flour

½ teaspoon baking powder

1 teaspoon bicarbonate of soda/baking soda

1 teaspoon ground cinnamon

3 teaspoons ground ginger

¼ teaspoon ground cloves

¼ teaspoon ground nutmeg

¼ teaspoon ground allspice

a pinch of cayenne pepper

a pinch of salt

125 g/1 stick unsalted butter, softened

75 g/⅓ cup soft/packed light brown sugar

1 egg, beaten

3 tablespoons clear honey

3 tablespoons molasses

1 tablespoon freshly squeezed lemon juice

Sift together the flour, baking powder, bicarbonate of soda/baking soda, spices and salt.

Cream together the butter and sugar until light and creamy. Add the beaten egg, honey, molasses and lemon juice and mix until smooth. Add the sifted dry ingredients and mix again until smooth. Knead the dough lightly, just enough to bring it together, then wrap in clingfilm/plastic wrap and refrigerate for 2 hours.

piping nozzles/tips and bags

If you plan on making lots of decorated cookies, it is worth considering investing in a selection of piping nozzles/tips in varying shapes and sizes. Piping bags also come in a variety of materials and sizes. Look out for easy-to-use disposable plastic piping bags that usually come in packs of 24 and can be trimmed either to a point or to fit most piping nozzles/tips.

how to make
2 paper piping bags

✳ Cut a large piece of baking parchment into a square. Fold the square in half diagonally, then cut along the fold to give you 2 triangles.

✳ Take 1 triangle. With the longest side closest to you, take the right-hand corner and turn it inwards towards the top corner to create the start of a cone. (1)

✳ Wrap the left-hand corner around the cone. (2)

✳ The left-hand corner should meet the top of the cone, underneath and facing the original, right-hand corner. Neaten the points so that you have a tight cone. (3)

✳ Flatten the cone – there will now be a triangle sticking out of the top. Fold this over a few times to secure the bag (4).

✳ Snip off the very tip. (5)

✳ Repeat to make another piping bag.

royal icing

This can easily be made using storebought royal icing sugar — simply follow the instructions on the pack. However, you can also make your own by following these instructions.

2 egg whites
500–600 g/4–4½ cups icing/
confectioners' sugar, sifted

Beat the egg whites until foamy using a wire whisk. Gradually add the sugar and whisk until the desired stiffness is reached – for piping, the icing should hold a solid ribbon trail. If you're not using it immediately, cover with clingfilm/plastic wrap.

To make shapes, fit a piping bag with the required nozzle/tip and fill with the royal icing. Line a baking sheet with baking parchment and pipe shapes onto the parchment. Set aside for at least 24 hours until set solid.

Shapes will keep for up to 1 week in an airtight container. Keep the shapes between layers of greaseproof/waxed paper.

storebought sugar paste, regal icing and ready-to-roll fondant

These 3 types of ready-made icings are available either in the baking aisle of most supermarkets or from sugarcraft suppliers (see page 63).

Sugar paste can be coloured using food colouring paste (see pages 14–15) and is ideal for rolling out to make shapes. It is usually used for more decorative items that need to set solid and dry quickly.

Regal icing or ready-made royal icing is slightly softer than sugar paste and can be coloured or flavoured using food colouring pastes and flavours.

Ready-to-roll fondant icing can be used for covering cookies and will set softer than royal or regal icing.

All of these icings are widely available in either white or ivory, but can also be found in a variety of colours from specialist sugarcraft suppliers.

chocolate glaze

A glossy, silky-smooth glaze for perfectly coating cookies.

300 g/9½ oz. dark/bittersweet chocolate, chopped
2 tablespoons sunflower or groundnut oil

Put the chocolate and oil in a heatproof bowl set over a pan of simmering water. Stir until smooth and thoroughly combined. Set aside to cool for about 10 minutes before using.

tinting royal icing

✳ Make some Royal Icing (page 12). Using a wooden skewer, cocktail stick or toothpick, add tiny amounts of food colouring paste to the icing. (1)

✳ Mix thoroughly before adding more colouring. Remember that some colours can intensify over time, so always add the colouring gradually, and in very small amounts. (2)

tinting fondant icing, sugar paste or marzipan

✳ Using a wooden skewer, cocktail stick or toothpick, add tiny amounts of food colouring paste to fondant icing, sugar paste or marzipan. (3)

✳ Knead until smooth and add more colouring accordingly. Remember that some colours can intensify over time so always add the colouring gradually, and in very small amounts.(4)

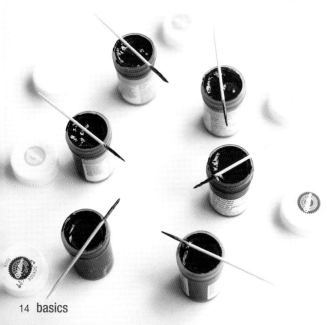

food colouring pastes

These are now widely available in sugarcraft and good kitchen stores and online from specialist cake decorating suppliers. They come in a rainbow of colours and can be used in tiny quantities without diluting your icing, making them much easier to work with than liquid colours.

embossing sugar paste and fondant icing

Embossing tools are a very effective way of creating simple, decorative patterns on either sugar paste or fondant icing. They can be bought from cake decorating stores and sugarcraft suppliers (see page 63). Alternatively, look around your kitchen and you may find some unlikely embossing tools: the fine side of a grater gently pressed into icing can create a delicate pattern; the underside of antique silver cutlery/flatware and the points of piping nozzles/tips can also make unusual shapes and designs.

other quick decorating ideas

✳ Look out for stencils in cake decorating stores or from sugarcraft suppliers. Made of plastic, they are available in a variety of designs and sizes. Dust either icing/confectioners' sugar, cocoa powder or edible coloured powders directly onto cookies.

✳ If you have patience and a steady hand, you could use a fine, soft brush to paint lustres onto fondant-covered cookies.

✳ Paper doilies make brilliant cheap and pretty stencils, and come in a variety of sizes and patterns. Alternatively, you could get creative with some paper and scissors and make your own stencil designs.

cute

Now there's a funny thing: a cookie that wants to be a cupcake — or is it a cupcake that wants to be a cookie? The particular cookie cutter used for this recipe is a cupcake topped with a candle. Gold leaf has been used for the flame here but you could simply paint it using food colouring pastes.

cupcake cookies

1 quantity Basic Vanilla Cookies
(page 8)

1 quantity Royal Icing (page 12)

pink food colouring paste

blue food colouring paste

pink, red and white sprinkles

edible gold leaf or dust (optional)

cupcake-shaped cookie cutter

*2 baking sheets, lined with baking
parchment*

*small piping bag with a fine
writing nozzle/tip, or make your
own (see page 11)*

mini palette knife or small knife

makes about 18

You should have rolled out the Basic Vanilla Cookie dough to a thickness
of 4 mm/⅛ inch on a lightly floured work surface. Using the cupcake cookie
cutter, carefully stamp out shapes. Arrange them on the prepared baking
sheets. Gather together the scraps of the dough and re-roll to make more
shapes. Refrigerate for 15 minutes.

Preheat the oven to 180°C (350°F) Gas 4.

Bake the cookies on the middle shelf of the preheated oven for about
12 minutes, or until golden, swapping the sheets around if needed.
Leave to cool on the sheets for about 5 minutes before transferring to
a wire rack to cool completely.

Divide the Royal Icing between 3 bowls. Tint one pink and one blue (see
page 14 for help on tinting) using the food colouring pastes. Tint them the
shade of pink or blue you like by very gradually adding more colouring.
Leave the third bowl of icing white.

Fill the piping bag with whichever colour you want to start with. Pipe
borders around the cold cookies. 'Flood' the area inside the borders with
icing (see page 22 for step pictures of 'flooding'): once you have made a
neat border, you can spoon icing within the borders and spread it carefully
up to the edges with a mini palette knife or small knife. Leave it to dry and
harden slightly before you pipe any lines on top of the flooded icing.
Decorate as you like with the sprinkles.

Attach a small piece of edible gold leaf to the flame of the candle with a
little brush. Allow to set before serving.

monogrammed wedding cookies

1 quantity Basic Vanilla Cookies
(page 8)

1 quantity Royal Icing (page 12)

blue food colouring paste (or
whichever colour you need for
your colour scheme)

*square, round and/or heart-
shaped cookie cutters*

*2 baking sheets, lined with baking
parchment*

*small piping bag with a fine
writing nozzle/tip, or make your
own (see page 11)*

mini palette knife or small knife

*makes about 12—18
depending on size*

You should have rolled out the Basic Vanilla Cookie dough to a thickness
of 4 mm/⅛ inch on a lightly floured work surface. Using the cookie cutters,
carefully stamp out shapes. Arrange them on the prepared baking sheets.
Gather together the scraps of the dough and re-roll to make more shapes.
Refrigerate for 15 minutes.

Preheat the oven to 180°C (350°F) Gas 4.

Bake the cookies on the middle shelf of the preheated oven for about
12 minutes, or until golden, swapping the sheets around if needed.
Leave to cool on the sheets for about 5 minutes before transferring to
a wire rack to cool completely.

Divide the Royal Icing between 2 bowls. Tint one blue (see page 14 for
help on tinting) using the food colouring paste. Leave the second bowl
of icing white.

Now see page 22 for instructions on how to decorate the cookies.

These cookies make beautiful wedding favours. They are best made from simple shapes: squares, rounds or hearts all work well. Frost the cookies in colours to match the wedding colour scheme and design. Why not personalize them for each guest and use as place settings?

how to decorate
monogrammed wedding cookies

✳ Fill the piping bag with whichever colour you want to start with. Pipe borders around the cold cookies. **(1)**

✳ Spoon icing within the borders and spread it carefully up to the edges with a mini palette knife or small knife. This is called 'flooding'. **(2)** Leave it to dry and harden slightly.

✳ Now fill your clean piping bag with the other colour of icing. Pipe lines, dots or other simple decorations on the cookies, then your chosen monogram in the centre. **(3)** Allow to set before serving.

cute 23

easter eggs and bunnies

1 quantity Basic Vanilla Cookies (page 8) or Gingerbread Cookies (page 9)

plain/all-purpose flour, for dusting

2 quantities Royal Icing (page 12)

brown food colouring paste

pink food colouring paste

blue food colouring paste

lilac food colouring paste

black food colouring paste

white nonpareils or sugar strands

easter egg-shaped cookie cutters

bunny rabbit-shaped cookie cutter

2 baking sheets, lined with baking parchment

small piping bag with a fine writing nozzle/tip, or make your own (see page 11)

mini palette knife or small knife

narrow checked ribbon (optional)

makes about 10–12 depending on size

If you haven't already done so, roll out the Basic Vanilla Cookie or Gingerbread Cookie dough to a thickness of 4 mm/⅛ inch on a lightly floured work surface. Using the cookie cutters, carefully stamp out egg and bunny shapes. Arrange them on the prepared baking sheets. Gather together the scraps of the dough and re-roll to make more shapes. Refrigerate for 15 minutes.

Preheat the oven to 180°C (350°F) Gas 4.

Bake the cookies on the middle shelf of the preheated oven for about 12 minutes, or until firm, swapping the sheets around if needed. Leave to cool on the sheets for about 5 minutes before transferring to a wire rack to cool completely.

Divide the Royal Icing between 6 bowls. Tint 5 of them a different colour (see page 14 for help on tinting) using the food colouring pastes. You will only need a tiny amount of black icing. Leave the last bowl of icing white.

Fill the piping bag with whichever colour you want to start with. Pipe borders around the cold egg-shaped cookies. 'Flood' the area inside the borders with icing (see page 22 for step pictures of 'flooding'): once you have made a neat border, you can spoon icing within the borders and spread it carefully up to the edges with a mini palette knife or small knife. Leave to dry and harden slightly before going any further.

Pipe in the rest of the design: draw lines, squiggles and dots over each egg. Set aside to dry completely.

Repeat the same technique for icing the bunnies using brown icing. Pipe in noses, mouths and eyes with the black icing. Finish off each rabbit with a fluffy tail: pipe a large blob of white icing in the correct position and scatter with the nonpareils or sugar strands.

Once the icing has completely set, tie a length of checked ribbon around the neck of each bunny and serve alongside the eggs.

Look for sets of assorted Easter-related cookie cutters, but if you can't find them, make paper templates, lay over the cookie dough, and carefully cut out using a small, sharp knife.

Look for images of Russian dolls and use them as templates for these cookies. Simply cut out the paper template, lay it onto the rolled-out cookie dough, and cut around it using a small, sharp knife.

russian dolls

1 quantity Basic Vanilla Cookies (page 8) or Gingerbread Cookies (page 9)

plain/all-purpose flour, for dusting

2 quantities Royal Icing (page 12)

red food colouring paste

black food colouring paste

red, pink and white heart- and star-shaped sugar sprinkles

russian doll-shaped paper templates

2 baking sheets, lined with baking parchment

small piping bag with a fine writing nozzle/tip, or make your own (see page 11)

mini palette knife or small knife

makes about 8–10 depending on size

If you haven't already done so, roll out the Basic Vanilla Cookie or Gingerbread Cookie dough to a thickness of 4 mm/⅛ inch on a lightly floured work surface. Lay your paper templates on top of the dough and cut around using a small, sharp knife. Arrange them on the prepared baking sheets. Gather together the scraps of the dough and re-roll to make more shapes. Refrigerate for 15 minutes.

Preheat the oven to 180°C (350°F) Gas 4.

Bake the cookies on the middle shelf of the preheated oven for 12 minutes, or until firm, swapping the sheets around if needed. Leave to cool on the sheets for 10 minutes before transferring to a wire rack to cool completely.

Divide the Royal Icing between 3 bowls. Tint one red and one black (see page 14 for help on tinting) using the food colouring pastes. Leave the third bowl of icing white.

Fill the piping bag with whichever colour you want to start with. Pipe borders around the cold cookies. If you want to make the 'belly' of the doll in the other colour of icing, you will need to create a border for this too. 'Flood' the area inside the borders with icing (see page 22 for step pictures of 'flooding'): once you have made a neat border, you can spoon icing within the borders and spread it carefully up to the edges with a mini palette knife or small knife. Leave to dry and harden slightly before going any further.

Pipe in the rest of the design and the dolls' faces. Now the fun starts: pipe small flowers, dots, squiggles and whatever you like over the dolls. Arrange the shaped sugar sprinkles all over. Allow to set before serving.

garden critters

1 quantity Basic Vanilla Cookies
(page 8)

1 quantity Royal Icing (page 12)

food colouring pastes in assorted
colours

*critter-shaped cookie cutters
(e.g. snail, ladybird, butterfly,
caterpillar)*

*2 baking sheets, lined with baking
parchment*

*small piping bag with a fine
writing nozzle/tip, or make your
own (see page 11)*

mini palette knife or small knife

*makes about 12—18
depending on size*

You should have rolled out the Basic Vanilla Cookie dough to a thickness
of 4 mm/⅛ inch on a lightly floured work surface. Using the critter cookie
cutters, carefully stamp out shapes. Arrange them on the prepared baking
sheets. Gather together the scraps of the dough and re-roll to make more
shapes. Refrigerate for 15 minutes.

Preheat the oven to 180°C (350°F) Gas 4.

Bake the cookies on the middle shelf of the preheated oven for about
12 minutes, or until golden, swapping the sheets around if needed.
Leave to cool on the sheets for about 5 minutes before transferring to
a wire rack to cool completely.

Divide the Royal Icing between the number of bowls you need for your
colours of icing. Tint each one a different colour (see page 14 for help on
tinting) using the food colouring pastes.

Fill the piping bag with whichever colour you want to start with. Pipe
borders around the cold cookies. 'Flood' the area inside the borders with
icing (see page 22 for step pictures of 'flooding'): once you have made a
neat border, you can spoon icing within the borders and spread it carefully
up to the edges with a mini palette knife or small knife.

Leave to dry and harden slightly before you pipe any lines or other features
on top of the flooded icing. Allow to set before serving.

Watch out! Here's an invasion of edible bugs and critters that kids will love to help decorate. Let them loose with the piping bag and food colouring (within reason!), and let them design their own critters.

man's best friend

They say that dogs are man's best friend… well now you can make yourself a whole new circle of friends! Choose your favourite breed and see if you can find a cookie cutter in the right shape from one of the suppliers on page 63.

1 quantity Basic Vanilla Cookies (page 8) or Gingerbread Cookies (page 9)

1 quantity Royal Icing (page 12)

food colouring pastes in assorted colours

dog-shaped cookie cutters

2 baking sheets, lined with baking parchment

small piping bag with a fine writing nozzle/tip, or make your own (see page 11)

mini palette knife or small knife

makes about 12—18 depending on size

If you haven't already done so, roll out the Basic Vanilla Cookie or Gingerbread Cookie dough to a thickness of 4 mm/⅛ inch on a lightly floured work surface. Lay your paper templates on top of the dough and cut around using a small, sharp knife. Arrange them on the prepared baking sheets. Gather together the scraps of the dough and re-roll to make more shapes. Refrigerate for 15 minutes.

Preheat the oven to 180°C (350°F) Gas 4.

Bake the cookies on the middle shelf of the preheated oven for 12 minutes, or until firm, swapping the sheets around if needed. Leave to cool on the sheets for 10 minutes before transferring to a wire rack to cool completely.

Divide the Royal Icing between the number of bowls you need for your colours of icing. Tint each one a different colour (see page 14 for help on tinting) using the food colouring pastes.

Fill the piping bag with whichever colour you want to start with. Pipe borders around the cold cookies. 'Flood' the area inside the borders with icing (see page 22 for step pictures of 'flooding'): once you have made a neat border, you can spoon icing within the borders and spread it carefully up to the edges with a mini palette knife or small knife.

Leave to dry and harden slightly before you pipe any lines or other features on top of the flooded icing. Allow to set before serving.

stained-glass cookies

These little cookies work best when made into simple shapes such as stars and flowers. The decoration is in the colourful 'stained-glass' centre, so the simpler the shape of the cookie, the more eye-catching the design. These are a great idea for children's parties — kids will love the pretty colours.

1 quantity Basic Vanilla Cookies (page 8)

1 bag fruit-flavoured boiled sweets/hard candies

selection of shaped cookie cutters

2 baking sheets, lined with baking parchment

makes about 24

You should have rolled out the Basic Vanilla Cookie dough to a thickness of 4 mm/⅛ inch on a lightly floured work surface. Using the cookie cutters, carefully stamp out shapes. Arrange them on the prepared baking sheets. Using smaller cutters, cut out a shape in the centre of each cookie. Gather together the scraps of the dough and re-roll to make more shapes. Refrigerate for 15 minutes.

Preheat the oven to 180°C (350°F) Gas 4.

Divide the boiled sweets/hard candies into separate colours and pop into plastic food bags. Using a rolling pin or mortar and pestle, crush the candies into small pieces.

Take the rolled cookies out of the refrigerator. Carefully fill the empty space in the centre of each cookie with the crushed sweets/candies in an even, thin layer and no thicker than the depth of the cookies.

Bake one baking sheet at a time on the middle shelf of the preheated oven for about 12 minutes, or until the cookies are pale golden and the candy has melted to fill the space.

Leave the cookies to cool on the sheets until the 'stained glass' has set.

This recipe makes approximately 12 cookies or 6 pairs of shoes, depending on the size of your cutters. Why not decorate the cookies to match your favourite outfit or to coordinate with a special event such as a girls' party or wedding?

a girl can never have enough shoes

1 quantity Basic Vanilla Cookies
(page 8) or Gingerbread Cookies
(page 9)

plain/all-purpose flour, for dusting

200–300 g/8–10 oz. white ready-
to-roll fondant icing or sugar paste

red food colouring paste

icing/confectioners' sugar,
for dusting

2 tablespoons sieved apricot jam,
warmed

pearly nonpareils

edible sugar diamonds (optional)

*high-heeled shoe-shaped cookie
cutter*

*2 baking sheets, lined with baking
parchment*

very small, round cookie cutter

embossing tools

makes about 6 pairs

If you haven't already done so, roll out the Basic Vanilla Cookie or
Gingerbread Cookie dough to a thickness of 4 mm/⅛ inch on a lightly
floured work surface. Using the shoe cookie cutter, carefully stamp out
shapes. Arrange them on the prepared baking sheets. Gather together
the scraps of the dough and re-roll to make more shapes. Refrigerate for
15 minutes.

Preheat the oven to 180°C (350°F) Gas 4.

Bake the cookies on the middle shelf of the preheated oven for about
12 minutes, or until firm, swapping the sheets around if needed. Leave to
cool on the sheets for about 5 minutes before transferring to a wire rack
to cool completely.

Divide the fondant icing (or sugar paste) into 2. Tint one portion red (see
page 14 for help on tinting) using the food colouring paste. Tint it the
shade of red you like by very gradually adding more colouring. Leave the
other half white.

Lightly dust a work surface with icing/confectioners' sugar. Roll out the
2 colours of fondant icing to a thickness of 2 mm/¹⁄₁₆ inch. Using the shoe
cookie cutter again, stamp out shoes to match each of your cookies. Using
the very small, round cookie cutter, stamp out circles all over each shoe.
Carefully remove the circles and reserve them.

Lightly brush the top of each cold cookie with the warmed apricot jam.
Carefully position one fondant shoe on top of each cookie, gently
smoothing into place with your hands. Use any scraps to make bows,
ribbons, and embellishments for your shoes. Take your little red reserved
circles and slot them into the holes in your white shoes. Repeat with the
white circles and red shoes. Stick the embellishments onto the shoes with
a tiny dab of cold water. Using embossing tools (see page 16), decorate
the shoes with patterns and gently press pearly nonpareils and/or sugar
diamonds into the designs. Allow to set before serving.

1 quantity Basic Vanilla Cookies (page 8)

200–300 g/8–10 oz. white ready-to-roll fondant icing

yellow food colouring paste

½ quantity Royal Icing (page 12)

black food colouring paste

icing/confectioners' sugar, for dusting

1 tablespoon sieved apricot jam, warmed

10–12-cm/4–5-inch sunflower-shaped cookie cutter

2 baking sheets, lined with baking parchment

small piping bag with a small star-shaped nozzle/tip

makes about 12 depending on size

sunflowers

These cookies are like a ray of sunshine on a gloomy day. Any type of flower-shaped cookie cutter can be used. Why not use a variety of shapes and sizes to make a flower cookie bouquet?

You should have rolled out the Basic Vanilla Cookie dough to a thickness of 4 mm/⅛ inch on a lightly floured work surface. Using the sunflower cookie cutter, carefully stamp out shapes. Arrange them on the prepared baking sheets. Gather together the scraps of the dough and re-roll to make more shapes. Refrigerate for 15 minutes.

Preheat the oven to 180°C (350°F) Gas 4.

Bake the cookies on the middle shelf of the preheated oven for about 12 minutes, or until golden, swapping the sheets around if needed. Leave to cool on the sheets for 5 minutes before transferring to a wire rack to cool completely.

Tint the fondant icing yellow (see page 14 for help on tinting) using the yellow food colouring paste and the Royal Icing black using the black food colouring paste.

Now see opposite for instructions on how to decorate the cookies.

how to decorate sunflowers

✳ Lightly dust a work surface with icing/confectioners' sugar. Roll out the yellow fondant icing to a thickness of 2 mm/⅟₁₆ inch.

✳ Using the cookie cutter, stamp out flowers to match the cookies. Brush the top of each cold cookie with the warmed apricot jam. Place a fondant flower on top of each cookie, gently smoothing into place with your hands. You may find it easier to transfer the fondant flower while still in the cutter.

✳ Fill the piping bag with the black royal icing and pipe rosettes into the middle of each sunflower.

✳ Allow to set before serving.

Gingerbread people come in a variety of shapes, sizes and states of undress!
You could make simple gingerbread men with their traditional decoration of
currant eyes and buttons, or go for something a little more unique such as
Adam and Eve, complete with fig leaves to protect their modesty.

gingerbread adam and eve

1 quantity Gingerbread Cookies
(page 9)

plain/all-purpose flour, for dusting

100 g/3½ oz. white ready-to-roll
fondant icing

green food colouring paste

icing/confectioners' sugar,
for dusting

*gingerbread man-shaped cookie
cutter*

*2 baking sheets, lined with baking
parchment*

*very small and medium flower-
shaped cutters*

*makes about 8—10
depending on size*

Preheat the oven to 180°C (350°F) Gas 4.

Take the Gingerbread Cookie dough out of the refrigerator and put it on a
lightly floured work surface. Roll it out to a thickness of 4 mm/⅛ inch. Using
the gingerbread man cookie cutter, carefully stamp out shapes. Arrange
them on the prepared baking sheets. Gather together the scraps of the
dough and re-roll to make more shapes.

Bake the cookies on the middle shelf of the preheated oven for about
10–12 minutes, or until firm and the edges are just starting to brown,
swapping the sheets around if needed. Leave to cool on the sheets for
about 5 minutes before transferring to a wire rack to cool completely.

If you'd like to make the white flowers as hair accessories for Eve, divide
the fondant icing into 2. (If you are only making fig leaves, you don't need
to divide it up.) Tint one portion green (see page 14 for help on tinting)
using the food colouring paste. Tint it the shade of green you like by very
gradually adding more colouring. Leave the other half white.

Lightly dust a work surface with icing/confectioners' sugar. Roll out the
2 colours of fondant icing to a thickness of 2 mm/¹⁄₁₆ inch. Cut out fig leaf
shapes with a small, sharp knife or use a paper template. Mark out the leaf
veins with the back of a knife. Stamp out flowers with the very small flower-
shaped cookie cutter for Eve's extra covering. To make flowers for Eve's
hair, use the medium flower-shaped cutter to stamp out however many you
need. Create lines on the flower petals with the back of a knife. Press the
flowers over the backs of spoons and leave them to dry out. Chop off tiny
pieces of the fondant and roll into balls for the centre of the flowers.

Stick the fig leaves, bikini flowers and hair accessories onto each cold
cookie in the correct position with a little dab of cold water!

snowflakes

1 quantity Gingerbread Cookies (page 9)

plain/all-purpose flour, for dusting

icing/confectioners' sugar, for dusting

200–300 g/8–10 oz. white ready-to-roll fondant icing

2 tablespoons sieved apricot jam, warmed

½ quantity Royal Icing (page 12)

silver and/or white edible glitter and nonpareils

snowflake cookie cutters in assorted shapes and sizes

2 baking sheets, lined with baking parchment

small piping bag with a fine writing nozzle/tip, or make your own (see page 11)

embossing tools (optional)

festive string or narrow ribbon (optional)

makes 12—16

Preheat the oven to 180°C (350°F) Gas 4.

Take the Gingerbread Cookie dough out of the refrigerator and put it on a lightly floured work surface. Roll it out to a thickness of 4 mm/⅛ inch. Using the snowflake cookie cutters, carefully stamp out shapes. Arrange them on the prepared baking sheets. Gather together the scraps of the dough and re-roll to make more shapes. If you are making these cookies to hang as Christmas decorations, using a wooden skewer, make a hole in the top of each snowflake big enough to push your ribbon through.

Bake the cookies on the middle shelf of the preheated oven for about 10–12 minutes, or until firm and the edges are just starting to brown, swapping the sheets around if needed. Leave to cool on the sheets for about 5 minutes before transferring to a wire rack to cool completely.

Lightly dust a work surface with icing/confectioners' sugar. Roll out the fondant icing to a thickness of no more than 4 mm/⅛ inch. Using the snowflake cookie cutters again, stamp out snowflakes to match each of your cookies. Lightly brush the top of each cold cookie with the warmed apricot jam. Carefully position one fondant snowflake on top of each cookie, gently smoothing into place with your hands.

Fill the piping bag with the Royal Icing and pipe a border around the edge of the fondant icing on each cookie. Decorate with lines and dots. While the royal icing is still wet, sprinkle edible glitter and nonpareils over it so that they stick in place.

Using embossing tools (see page 16), press decorative patterns into the fondant icing, if you like. If you have made holes in the cookies to hang them, you will need to push the skewer into the fondant to make a hole in the same place. Leave the cookies to dry, then push a length of string or ribbon through each hole and tie a knot to secure.

Look for snowflake cookie cutters in sets of assorted shapes and sizes. Once covered in fondant icing, these cookies can be decorated in a vast array of nonpareils and glitter, which all help to create that festive, frosty feel.

black and white cookies

These elegant cookies are a breeze to make and wouldn't look out of place at the smartest tea table.

175 g/1⅓ cups plain/all-purpose flour, plus extra for dusting

50 g/½ cup cocoa powder

½ teaspoon baking powder

½ teaspoon bicarbonate of soda/baking soda

a pinch of salt

125 g/1 stick unsalted butter, softened

225 g/1 generous cup caster sugar

1 egg, beaten

1 teaspoon vanilla extract

100 g/3½ oz. white chocolate, chopped

1 quantity Chocolate Glaze (page 13)

5-cm/2-inch and 7-cm/3-inch round cookie cutters

2 baking sheets, lined with baking parchment

small piping bag with a fine writing nozzle/tip, or make your own (see page 11)

mini palette knife or small knife

Sift together the flour, cocoa powder, baking powder, bicarbonate of soda/baking soda and salt into a mixing bowl.

Cream together the butter and sugar until light and creamy in the bowl of a freestanding mixer (or use an electric whisk and mixing bowl). Add the beaten egg and vanilla and mix well. Add the sifted dry ingredients and mix again until smooth. Bring together into a dough and knead very lightly and briefly. Flatten into a disc, wrap in clingfilm/plastic wrap, and refrigerate for a couple of hours until very firm.

Preheat the oven to 180°C (350°F) Gas 4.

Dust the work surface with flour and roll out the chilled cookie dough to a thickness of about 4 mm/⅛ inch. Using the cookie cutters, carefully stamp out rounds. Arrange them on the prepared baking sheets. Gather together the scraps of the dough and re-roll to make more rounds.

Bake on the middle shelf of the preheated oven for 12–15 minutes, or until crisp. Leave to cool on the sheets for a couple of minutes before transferring to a wire rack to cool completely.

To decorate the cookies, put the white chocolate in a heatproof bowl set over a pan of barely simmering water. Stir until smooth and thoroughly melted. Put the cookies back on some baking parchment to catch any drips while you are decorating them.

Fill your piping bag with the molten white chocolate and get a wooden skewer, cocktail stick or toothpick ready for the feathering.

Now see overleaf for instructions on how to decorate the cookies.

makes about 16

1

2

The feathering technique is useful to know because it can be used for royal icing as well as this chocolate glaze. Feel free to be as expressive as you like with the flourishes.

3

how to decorate black and white cookies

✳ Pour some of the Chocolate Glaze over each cookie with a spoon (1).

✳ Spread the glaze neatly over the cookie, just to the edge, with the back of the spoon or with a mini palette knife. Repeat with the remaining cookies (2).

✳ Working quickly, pipe dots of white chocolate over the chocolate glaze on a few of the cookies (3).

✳ Using a wooden skewer, drag the white chocolate into the chocolate glaze to create a feathered effect. Repeat with the remaining cookies and allow to set before serving (4).

mint chocolate kisses

175 g/6 oz. dark/bittersweet chocolate, chopped

175 g/12 tablespoons unsalted butter

2 medium eggs

225 g/1 generous cup packed light muscovado sugar

250 g/2 cups self-raising flour

¾ teaspoon baking powder

a pinch of salt

minty buttercream

75 g/5 tablespoons unsalted butter, softened

150 g/1 cup icing/confectioners' sugar, sifted

½–1 teaspoon peppermint extract

to decorate

200 g/6½ oz. dark/bittersweet chocolate, chopped

hundreds and thousands/jimmies

2 baking sheets, lined with baking parchment

makes about 18

Put the chocolate and butter in a heatproof bowl set over a pan of barely simmering water. Stir until smooth and thoroughly combined.

Put the eggs and sugar in the bowl of a freestanding electric mixer fitted with the whisk attachment (or use an electric whisk and mixing bowl) and beat until pale and light. Add the chocolate mixture and mix until smooth.

Sift together the flour, baking powder and salt. Add to the mixing bowl and stir until smooth. Bring together into a dough, cover and refrigerate for a couple of hours.

Preheat the oven to 180°C (350°F) Gas 4.

Remove the cookie dough from the refrigerator and pull off walnut-sized pieces. Roll into balls and arrange on the prepared baking sheets. Bake in batches on the middle shelf of the preheated oven for about 12 minutes, or until the cookies are crisp on the edges but slightly soft in the middle. Leave to cool on the sheets for a few minutes before transferring to a wire rack to cool completely.

To make the minty buttercream, put the butter in a large bowl and, using a freestanding mixer or electric whisk, cream until really soft. Gradually add the sifted icing/confectioners' sugar and beat until pale and smooth. Add peppermint to taste.

Sandwich the cold cookies together with the minty buttercream.

To decorate, put the chocolate in a heatproof bowl set over a pan of barely simmering water. Stir until smooth and melted. Leave to cool slightly. Half-dip the cookies in the melted chocolate, sprinkle with hundreds and thousands/jimmies and allow to set on baking parchment before serving.

This is the kind of treat to put a smile on your face — it has something to do with the nostalgic combination of chocolate, peppermint and sprinkles.

This simple shortbread can be adapted into a variety of flavours and colours. Match the colour of the sugar to the flavour of the cookies: yellow for lemon, green for pistachio, and purple for lavender. Decide on one flavour and corresponding colour scheme before you start.

sugared refrigerator cookies

225 g/15 tablespoons unsalted butter, softened

125 g/⅔ cup caster sugar

1 egg, beaten

1 teaspoon vanilla extract

300 g/2⅓ cups plain/all-purpose flour, plus extra for dusting

a pinch of salt

4 tablespoons granulated sugar

yellow, red, green and/or purple food colouring pastes to match your colour scheme

1 tablespoon milk

one flavouring of your choice

2 tablespoons finely chopped mixed peel or 125 g/4 oz. chopped glacé cherries or 125 g/ 4 oz. chopped pistachios or 2 tablespoons dried lavender flowers, to match your colour scheme

2 baking sheets, lined with baking parchment

makes about 20

Cream together the butter and sugar until light and creamy in the bowl of a freestanding mixer (or use an electric whisk and mixing bowl). Add the egg and vanilla and mix well. Sift the flour and salt into the mixture, along with the flavouring you have chosen, and mix again until smooth and the flour is incorporated.

Tip the dough onto a very lightly floured work surface and divide into 2. Roll each piece of dough into a sausage shape roughly 5 cm/2 inches in diameter, wrap tightly in greaseproof/waxed paper and refrigerate until solid – at least 2 hours.

Preheat the oven to 150°C (300°F) Gas 3.

Tip the granulated sugar into a plastic food bag. Using the tip of a wooden skewer, gradually add the colour of food colouring paste you have chosen to match the flavour of the cookie, mixing well until the desired shade is reached. Tip the coloured sugar onto a baking sheet. Remove the cookie dough logs from the refrigerator and brush them with the milk. Roll in the coloured sugar to coat evenly.

Using a sharp knife, cut the logs into 5-mm/³⁄₁₆-inch slices and arrange on the prepared baking sheets. Bake on the middle shelf of the preheated oven for about 15 minutes, or until pale golden. Leave to cool on the sheets for 5 minutes before transferring to a wire rack to cool completely.

classic oat cookies

These cookies are always popular, whether plain or flavoured with dried fruit or spices. Use old-fashioned porridge oats or rolled oats rather than 'instant'.

115 g/1 stick unsalted butter, very soft

140 g/¾ cup packed light muscovado/brown sugar

1 egg, beaten

1 tablespoon milk

½ teaspoon vanilla extract

100 g/¾ cup plus 1 tablespoon self-raising flour

150 g/1½ cups rolled oats/coarse oatmeal

2 baking sheets, lightly greased

makes about 24

Preheat the oven to 180°C (350°F) Gas 4.

Put the butter, sugar, egg, milk and vanilla in the bowl of a freestanding mixer (or use an electric whisk and mixing bowl) and beat well. Add the flour and oats and mix well with a wooden spoon.

Put heaped teaspoons of dough onto the prepared baking sheets, spacing them well apart.

Bake in the preheated oven for 12–15 minutes, until lightly browned around the edges. Leave to cool on the sheets for a couple of minutes before transferring to a wire rack to cool completely.

Variations

At the same time as the flour, add either:
• 75 g/½ cup dried fruit (raisins, cherries, cranberries or blueberries)
• 1 teaspoon ground cinnamon, 1 teaspoon mixed spice/apple pie spice and 2 pinches of ground black pepper
• 60 g/⅓ cup chocolate chips and 25 g/¼ cup chopped almonds.

simple

extra-crunchy peanut butter cookies

For the best flavour, use a good-quality peanut butter with no added sugar. The crunchy coating is made by rolling the cookie mixture in roasted (but unsalted) peanuts before baking.

115 g/1 stick unsalted butter, softened

125 g/½ cup crunchy peanut butter

140 g/¾ cup packed light muscovado/brown sugar

1 egg, lightly beaten

½ teaspoon vanilla extract

225 g/1½ cups self-raising flour

200 g/1⅓ cups roasted unsalted peanut halves

2 baking sheets, greased

makes about 20

Preheat the oven to 180°C (350°F) Gas 4.

Put the butter, peanut butter, sugar, egg, vanilla and flour in a large bowl. Mix well with a wooden spoon.

Take walnut-sized portions of the dough (about a tablespoon) and roll into balls with your hands. Put the peanut halves in a shallow dish, then roll the dough in the nuts. Arrange the balls well apart on the prepared sheets, then gently flatten slightly with your fingers.

Bake in the preheated oven for 12–15 minutes, until light golden brown. Leave to cool on the sheets for a couple of minutes before transferring to a wire rack to cool completely.

Always popular and hard to beat! The classic recipe has been adapted so that it uses less sugar and more nuts. You can either use chocolate chips or a bar of chocolate broken up into chunks.

classic chocolate chip cookies

175 g/1⅓ cups self-raising flour

a pinch of salt

a good pinch of bicarbonate of soda/baking soda

115 g/1 stick unsalted butter, very soft

60 g/a scant ⅓ cup caster sugar

60 g/⅓ cup packed light muscovado/brown sugar

½ teaspoon vanilla extract

1 egg, lightly beaten

175 g/1 cup dark/bittersweet chocolate chips

75 g/¾ cup walnut or pecan pieces

2 baking sheets, greased

makes about 24

Preheat the oven to 190°C (375°F) Gas 5.

Put all the ingredients in a large bowl and mix well with a wooden spoon.

Drop heaped teaspoons of the mixture onto the prepared sheets, spacing them well apart.

Bake in the preheated oven for 8–10 minutes, until lightly coloured and just firm. Leave to cool on the sheets for a couple of minutes before transferring to a wire rack to cool completely.

double chocolate and pecan cookies

Good-quality chocolate is mixed into these cookies as chunks and as a powder (by simply processing with the flour).

100 g/1 cup rolled oats/coarse oatmeal

140 g/1¼ cups plain/all-purpose flour

½ teaspoon baking powder

½ teaspoon bicarbonate of soda/baking soda

85 g/½ cup packed light muscovado/brown sugar

200 g/7 oz. dark/bittersweet chocolate, broken up

115 g/1 stick unsalted butter, very soft

1 egg, beaten

100 g/1 cup pecan pieces

2 baking sheets, greased

makes about 24

Preheat the oven to 190°C (375°F) Gas 5.

Put the oats in a food processor. Add the flour, baking powder, bicarbonate of soda/baking soda, the sugar and half of the chocolate pieces. Process until the mixture has a sandy texture.

Put the butter, egg, pecan pieces and the remaining pieces of chocolate in a large bowl. Add the mixture from the processor and mix well with a wooden spoon or your hands to make a firm dough.

Roll walnut-sized pieces of dough into balls using your hands. Arrange well apart on the prepared baking sheets and flatten slightly with the back of a fork.

Bake in the preheated oven for 12–15 minutes, until almost firm. Leave to cool on the sheets for a couple of minutes before transferring to a wire rack to cool completely.

The original mocha was a fine Arabian coffee shipped from a port in Yemen called Mocha. Now the word means either a hot drink made of coffee and chocolate together, or other sweet mixtures using these two flavours. These little cookies are perfect with a cup of coffee after dinner.

mocha kisses

180 g/1⅓ cups self-raising flour

90 g/½ cup caster sugar

90 g/6 tablespoons unsalted butter, chilled and cubed

2 teaspoons instant coffee granules or powder

1 egg

filling

75 g/5 tablespoons unsalted butter, very soft

150 g/1¼ icing/confectioners' sugar

2 teaspoons instant coffee granules or powder

2 teaspoons cocoa powder

2 baking sheets, greased

makes about 9

Preheat the oven to 160°C (325°F) Gas 3.

If making the dough by hand, mix the flour and sugar in a bowl. Add the pieces of butter and, using the tips of your fingers, rub in until the mixture looks like breadcrumbs. Put the coffee in a bowl and dissolve in 1 teaspoon of warm water. Add the egg and beat lightly. Stir the egg and coffee mixture into the flour mixture with a wooden spoon. Mix well so that the ingredients come together to make a firm dough.

Alternatively, put the flour, sugar and pieces of butter in a food processor. Process until the mixture looks like breadcrumbs. Add the egg, then the coffee dissolved in a teaspoon of warm water. Process until the dough comes together. Carefully remove from the machine.

Flour your hands and roll the dough into 18 walnut-sized balls and arrange them slightly apart on the prepared baking sheets.

Bake in the preheated oven for 10–15 minutes, until a light golden colour. Leave to cool on the sheets for a couple of minutes before transferring to a wire rack to cool completely.

Meanwhile, to make the filling, put the butter, sugar, coffee and cocoa in a bowl and beat well with a wooden spoon or electric whisk – there will be flecks of coffee in the smooth icing. Use to sandwich the cookies in pairs.

suppliers and stockists

UK

The Cook's Kitchen
http://thecookskitchen.com
Tel: +44 (0)844 3574772
Suppliers of decorating tools such as stencils and embossing tools.

Design a Cake
www.design-a-cake.co.uk
Tel: +44 (0)191 417 1572
Large selection of sugarcraft and baking items including stencils.

H. O. Foose Tinsmithing
See below.

Jane Asher
www.jane-asher.co.uk
Tel: +44 (0)20 7584 6177
Wide range of cake baking and decorating supplies, including tiny cutters and embossing tools.

Lakeland
www.lakeland.co.uk
Tel: +44 (0)1539 488 100
Huge selection of baking equipment, plus flower-shaped cutters in a range of sizes.

Lindy's Cakes
www.lindyscakes.co.uk
Tel: +44 (0)1296 622 418
Sugarcraft and cake baking items including embossing sticks.

Make a Wish!
www.makeawishcakeshop.co.uk
Huge selection of cake decorating items: sugar flowers, tiny cutters, pretty ribbons and much more.

Squires Kitchen
www.squires-shop.com
Tel: +44 (0)845 22 55 671
Large retailer of cake decorating and sugarcraft supplies, eg edible gold and silver leaf and assorted shoe-shaped cookie cutters!

US

Crate & Barrel
www.crateandbarrel.com
Tel: +1 800 967 6696
Store and online supplier of kitchenware.

H. O. Foose Tinsmithing
www.foosecookiecutters.com
More than 700 hand-made cookie cutters. If you can't find what you're looking for on this site you can buy kits to make up your own designs.

Karen's Cookies
www.karenscookies.net
Tel: +1 800 934 3997
Cutters in the shape of high-heeled shoes, different breeds of dog, critters and flowers.

Kitchen Krafts
www.kitchenkrafts.com
Tel: +1 800 298 5389
Bakeware, decorating tools and ready-made icings, cookie cutters, piping bags and nozzles/tips.

Sugarcraft
www.sugarcraft.com
Every type of cake decoration imaginable, plus useful boxes for presenting and carrying cookies.

Sur la Table
www.surlatable.com
Tel: +1 800 243 0852
Bakeware including cupcake cookie cutters and piping bags and nozzles/tips. Good for speciality ingredients, eg fondant and fondant icing sugar.

Wilton
www.wilton.com
Baking and decorating supplies eg sprinkles and food colouring.

index